KT-364-699

THE HEROINE OF NEWGATE

The Story of Elizabeth Fry

by
JOHN MILSOME

LUTTERWORTH PRESS
Cambridge

For Isobel

**Lutterworth Press
7 All Saints' Passage
Cambridge CB2 3LS**

British Library Cataloguing in Publication Data

Milsome, John
Heroine of Newgate: the story of Elizabeth
Fry.—(Stories of faith and fame).
1. Fry, Elizabeth—Juvenile literature
2. Prison reformers—Great Britain—
Biography—Juvenile literature
I. Title   II. Series
365′.7′0924   HV8978.F7

ISBN 0-7188-2677-9

Cover illustration by Elissa Vial
Copyright © Lutterworth Press 1987
First published 1987 by Lutterworth Press

All rights reserved. No part of this publication may be reproduced, stored in a retrieval system, or transmitted in any form or by any means, electronic, mechanical, photocopying, recording, or otherwise, without the prior permission in writing of the publisher.

Typeset in Monophoto Plantin Medium by
Vision Typesetting, Manchester

Made and printed in Great Britain by
The Guernsey Press Co. Ltd., Guernsey, Channel Islands.

THE HEROINE OF NEWGATE

Elizabeth Fry (1780–1845) from an early age felt the need to help the poor and suffering. Her work to relieve the terrible conditions for women prisoners in Newgate Prison and those being transported to Australia has made her famous. Her life story demonstrates her great courage.

STORIES OF FAITH AND FAME

CONTENTS

1

THE GURNEYS OF NORWICH

"I DO wish our Betsy would concentrate on her lessons," said Catherine Gurney as she watched her quiet, fair haired little daughter being teased by her brothers and sisters. "They're making fun of her spelling again."

"I think her illness has taken away some of her energy," said her husband, John Gurney. "Betsy will make her mark in the world one day I'm sure and I hope we are still here to see it."

Elizabeth Gurney, known as Betsy by her family and friends, had been born on 21 May 1780 in her parents' home, the Court House, in Magdalen Street, Norwich. She had two older sisters, Kitty born in 1776 and Rachel in 1777. Eventually they were to be part of a very large family of seven girls and four boys. Of these, Betsy had always been thought of as the quiet and slow one, not so strong as her brothers and sisters.

Her father was a member of the Society of Friends or Quakers, a religious sect founded by George Fox, a shoemaker and herdsman who lived in the 17th century. Members met in a simple room and observed a long silence before anyone spoke. They wore plain clothing and tried to follow an honest and hard-working life.

Many of them were good business men who prospered through sound trading methods. Although John Gurney was a Quaker, he was not as strict as some and allowed his daughters to wear colourful clothes and to enjoy themselves at parties and dances.

John Gurney was a successful business man and banker with enough wealth to rent a small country house at Bramerton, a few miles from Norwich. Here he could enjoy the peace of the countryside and his children could see interesting animals, trees and flowers. Betsy was a nervous child, often scared of the remote, wild and dark corners of the garden of this country house.

"Let's come and explore together," her mother would say, taking Betsy's hand so that the child would lose her fear.

Sometimes the family visited Cromer where the children loved the beach, though Betsy did not share their love for the sea and hated to go near it. The sound of the distant waves was enough to make her cry. When her brothers and sisters shouted, "Come into the sea with us Betsy," there were more floods of tears.

Betsy was also apprehensive of the night. She would go to bed, only to wake up and find her night light had gone out and she was all alone in the dark. Her mother would come and find her daughter awake and in tears. She tried to re-assure her and read her stories from the Bible to calm her but Betsy's fears remained.

By the time John and Catherine Gurney had a

family of ten children, they decided that the house at Magdalen Street was not big enough for them. They therefore moved to Earlham Hall, a large 17th century mansion, only two miles from Norwich but with fine lawns and stables. It was a place where the lively and unruly Gurney children could enjoy horse riding and boating and all except Betsy were delighted to go there.

As soon as Betsy saw the great building of red brick and flint, she wanted to run away. It looked strange, high and forbidding with its bays and star shaped windows. She was even more scared when she went inside. There were so many rooms that she was sure she would be lost if she dared to leave her family and wander about alone. There were winding staircases that seemed to go on for ever and so many closets and cupboards where strange things might lurk, that she lost count. In years to come though, she was to love this house.

Shouting, making fun of everybody in sight and climbing into forbidden places were second nature to the Gurney children who were known in Norwich for their unruly behaviour. Earlham Hall offered plenty of space for this energetic family, and all the children, even Betsy, loved to play both inside and outside their new home. If Betsy was in tears, her older sister Rachel would try to comfort her. Rachel seemed so kindly and fearless that Betsy often went to her when she was scared.

The girls could, if they wished, ride their ponies in the spacious grounds around their home. In this, Betsy was no different. She loved her pony and could match her brothers and sisters in riding skill. They often rode into Norwich, then a large country town linked to London by mail coach. There was a lot of fun to be had in Norwich, watching the coaches arriving and leaving and listening to the town band. Perhaps, best of all, they loved to dress in fine clothes for their visits there.

Back home at Earlham Hall, they would share the pleasures of picnics, when they roasted potatoes in fires they had made. Then there were a host of games they could play under the trees. Betsy would try to join in but her poor health meant that she did not have the energy of the others. Games of hide-and-seek would usually end with her being the first to be caught, so she was often left out of the games.

At the end of the day, they all wrote up their diaries, sometimes confessing how badly they had behaved. Louisa was the worst, frequently describing how nurse had scolded her but Rachel too, admitted that she enjoyed being rude. They particularly enjoyed playing a trick on their cousin, Hudson Gurney, when he visited Earlham Hall.

Betsy had seen Hudson and spoken to him but later he seemed to have left. When she asked her sisters where he was, they giggled and pretended that they didn't know.

"The last time we saw him, he was looking for the pantry," said Louisa.

There were squeals of laughter from the girls

and seeing Betsy's puzzled expression, Kitty went to the pantry door.

"I do believe I can hear somebody knocking," she said.

There was more loud laughter from the girls. Then Kitty unlocked the key on the outside and as Betsy stood watching, her sisters ran away, their cries of laughter fading into the distance. The door of the pantry suddenly opened and Hudson came out.

"You just wait," he said. "I'll get my own back on those sisters of yours."

It is unlikely that he ever did manage to get his own back on those lively, mischievous girls but equally possible that Betsy scolded them for their silly behaviour.

When they weren't playing tricks, horse riding and boating on the River Wensum, the girls were expected to work very hard at their lessons. They had to be up early in the morning, ready for two hours of lessons before breakfast. Their mother had arranged for visiting teachers to come to their home to teach art, French, mathematics and many other subjects. The older boys, John and Samuel, were away at boarding school but a visiting governess and nurse looked after the very young boys.

At mid-day lessons stopped while the children had their lunch. There were more lessons until three o'clock when there was another break for dinner. Then came yet more lessons until tea at six o'clock. No wonder that after this the girls were ready to escape into the gardens and ride their ponies.

As they were Quakers they had to go to the Society of Friends Meeting House in Norwich every Sunday. The Gurney girls were better off than the others at the meeting and their colourful and more expensive clothes showed this. The old Meeting House was in Goats Lane and Betsy and her sisters always called the place "Goats".

At the Sunday Meeting the Gurney sisters had to sit quiet for long periods and then listen to what seemed to them boring sermons. The girls found much of the Sunday Meeting uninteresting. Betsy, too, found it hard to sit still and was always glad to escape with her sisters to Earlham Hall.

When Betsy was ten, her mother had her twelfth child, Daniel. One day in March 1791 Betsy was studying with her sisters, Rachel and Catherine, when the maid came into their room. She told them that their mother had just given birth to a baby boy. Catherine then called all the younger sisters from the garden and led them in a long procession into their mother's room. Very quietly they gazed at the new baby Daniel. It was a happy moment they all shared.

For the next two years life for the Gurney children was full of music, dancing and fun, although Betsy still remained apart from the others. Even as a child she thought about her life and wondered how she could improve it. Many interesting people came to Earlham Hall and Betsy and her sisters had opportunities to talk to them. On these occasions she was often outshone by her brighter, older sisters.

In October 1792 Mrs Gurney became ill. The doctor came often to the house and the children had to be very quiet. Although she was weak and supposed to be in bed, Mrs Gurney insisted on getting up each day to conduct prayers with her family.

Her oldest daughter Kitty promised her mother that she would always look after all the other children. On 17 November Mrs Gurney died and, true to her word, fifteen year old Kitty took on the role of mother to the Gurney family. She had to help her father and watch over the servants and nurse who had all been with the family for some time. They tried to be helpful in return. It was only eleven year old Betsy who found it difficult to help at this time. Betsy, the odd one out, the nervous one in the family had been used to going to her mother when she was unhappy.

"Where's Betsy this morning?" Kitty asked her sisters.

"She's late because it's her Latin lesson, which she hates," said Rachel.

At that moment Betsy came hurrying into the room. She sat down with her Latin book, opened it and pretended to study.

"You must get here on time," said Kitty. "This isn't the first occasion this week that you've been late."

"I don't feel very well," replied Betsy, her lips trembling as she fought back the tears.

"Betsy, you were late for French several times last week and you were warned that if you were late again, you'd have to speak only French on your walks to Norwich. So if you are heard speaking English on your walk this evening, you will have to pay a farthing fine." Such punishments made Betsy resentful and moody.

At sixteen Betsy was a tall, pleasant looking girl but she was still often unhappy and did not get on well with her sisters. It was at that time that she met a young man named James Lloyd, a Quaker whose father had founded Lloyds Bank. While James was staying at Earlham Hall he became very fond of Betsy. They were engaged but there must have been some disagreement for they never married.

In general, life for the Gurney family was a pleasant routine but there were occasional excitements. In April 1797 Prince William Frederick, the nephew of King George III, was stationed with his army unit at Norwich. At that time, John Gurney, as an important local business man, was invited to dine with the Prince. The invitation included his seven daughters. The Prince was young and found the Gurney girls attractive company and the dinner was a great success.

The result was an eventual invitation to Prince William to come to Earlham Hall. The girls were very excited and delighted when the Prince accepted the invitation. They were waiting in their finest dresses when he arrived in his royal coach. Naturally it was exciting for them to talk with him and for his part the Prince liked their natural and friendly manner.

Prince William so enjoyed his visit that he didn't worry about the time and stayed two hours longer than had been expected. He was to meet the Gurney family at other times during that year and he always found these occasions very happy ones.

Betsy had been as excited as her sisters at meeting royalty and wrote in her diary, "My mind feels flat after a storm of pleasure." There were some Gurney relatives however who did not approve of all the fuss, fun and frivolity caused by the visit of the Prince. One of these was Uncle Joseph who wrote to John Gurney telling him that it was wrong for him as a Quaker to invite a royal prince to his home. John's reply was to ask Uncle Joseph to come to Earlham to meet the Prince.

Some time after the visit, Betsy began to have doubts about the royal visits. She felt there was something false about such occasions, exciting though they were. She believed there must be more to life than just dressing up in fine clothes and having a good time. At first she was not sure what it was that was lacking from her life but in time she realised that for her it was religion. She wrote in her diary at the end of 1797, "A thought passed my mind that if I had some religion, I should be superior to what I am."

At Christmas that year Prince William was again a guest at Earlham Hall, joining in the carol singing round the fire. When he called again about two weeks later, Louisa wrote in her diary that Rachel had amused them by giving a mock Quaker sermon. As Betsy was not mentioned it is possible that she was tiring of royal visits. In the past she had shown that she could dance and join in the fun when she wished. Now she was longing for something more worthwhile to do and wrote in her diary, "I am now seventeen, and if some kind circumstance does not happen to me I shall have my talents devoured by moth and rust."

Then something did happen that brought a great change to her life. John Gurney began to take notice of the criticisms of his strict Quaker brother, Joseph. He now encouraged his children to follow the Quaker way of living and this meant a more serious attitude and regular attendance at Meeting.

On 3 February 1798 an American Quaker named William Savery came to Norwich. He had been conducting a kind of Quaker mission of faith and peace in Europe and had arrived in Britain to continue his work. The Gurney girls were not especially keen to go but were persuaded to have second thoughts when Rachel read a report from her father's newspaper.

"This American sounds a very unusual and interesting man," she said.

"What's so wonderful about him?" asked Betsy. "Most of the speakers we hear at Meeting are boring."

But the other girls were attracted by what Rachel was saying. Savery spoke foreign languages and had travelled to many countries. He had even been to the western parts of America where he had preached to an audience of Red Indians. As usual with well known and successful Quakers, he was a wealthy business man and a strong believer in simple dress and way of life.

"Whatever you do Betsy, I am going to Meeting to hear William Savery," said Rachel.

The other girls agreed with her, leaving Betsy undecided. In the end she changed her mind to the extent that she reluctantly agreed to go with them, possibly because she knew that this was what her father wanted.

"Perhaps you're right," she said. "He might be more interesting than most people we hear there although I doubt whether he'll make much impression on me."

So the Gurney girls pleased their father by going to Meeting—in their fine colourful dresses that made them stand out from the large crowd of plainly clothed Quakers. Even Betsy wore her new purple boots with red laces. She sat in the front row where she could be seen by the speaker.

William Savery was a plump man of forty-eight, wearing typical plain Quaker clothing. He noticed Betsy and her sisters at once and was not impressed by their showy appearance. He certainly thought they were no example for young Quaker women to follow. For their part the girls could hardly have been impressed by this ordinary looking middle aged American but when he spoke they soon changed their minds.

After the usual long silence had been observed,

William Savery stood up and started to speak in his pleasant American accent. He had a way of speaking that made everyone listen. Although there had been years of war and revolution in France, Savery talked of peace and the need for religion and faith in God. He was so sincere and his message was so important that the Gurney girls found themselves listening with great attention. To Betsy especially, Savery had things to say about religion that changed her way of thinking.

For three hours Savery talked and held the interest of his audience all that time. On their way back in the carriage, Betsy talked to her sisters about the American Quaker. Her sister Richenda noticed that Betsy had been in tears and the other girls made fun of her but she soon silenced them when she praised the way Savery had spoken and described the great religious effect he had on her.

That evening there was another long Meeting and this time Betsy was taken in the coach by her Uncle Joseph, and William Savery travelled with them. She was able to talk to the American in the coach and listen to him preach again at Meeting. William Savery was then invited to Earlham Hall by Betsy's father. The American especially noticed how John Gurney's children were kind and attentive to him and what a fine library the house had.

When William Savery left Norwich, Betsy felt she had gone through a religious experience that had given her a new purpose in life. This made her discontented and she quarrelled with her sisters. They had quickly forgotten the words spoken by Savery the first time they had heard him and Betsy could not understand how they could do this. She thought they were silly and too easily pleased with their lives, but they thought she was too bossy, straight-laced and unfriendly with no sense of fun.

Their father noticed how Betsy did not get on with her sisters. He was going to London in February 1798 to deal with some business.

"I've never seen London although I am eighteen years of age," said Betsy.

"Then why don't you come with me? You could stay with your aunt and uncle and visit other cousins and friends."

"I'd be delighted to do that," said Betsy.

This was true. Betsy had felt restless and hoped this could be changed by a journey and a chance to stay in a huge and strange city and see new sights. She knew her father would have to be away from London for some of the time but Betsy loved her independence. For the first time she would experience a new kind of freedom. She could hardly wait for the day when she would board the mail coach at Norwich and travel south to London.

Some rattling old stage coaches still ran between large towns but the mail coaches, with their better springs, offered more comfort and a faster journey. The fare from Norwich to London was one pound six shillings for inside passengers and sixteen shillings for those willing to travel outside and risk the freezing rain. It was an expensive journey, especially for those who travelled inside the coach.

In the past when the Gurney sisters had watched the coaches in Norwich, Betsy had looked out for horses she especially liked. Their working life was about four years. An average journey in a day was fifty miles. During this time there would be a number of brief stops to change horses. Then the passengers would be able to recover from the constant jolting of the coach and have something to eat and drink. The sound of a warning blast on the guard's horn alerted other vehicles to get out of the way as the coach was leaving.

Betsy had been on shorter trips to places near Norwich but the journey to London of over one hundred miles was something new and exciting. It would take fourteen hours. The first stage of the journey was fifty miles to an inn just outside Newmarket. There was much discontent and unrest in the country, and the prospect of passing through unknown villages and towns made Betsy feel nervous as the day of departure approached. But she was very excited, too, about the chance to see the great capital city of London.

She wrote in her diary, "My mind is in a whirl. In all probability I shall be going to London . . . I must be careful not to get vain or silly."

2

JOSEPH FRY

"DON'T worry young lady, there's not a miller among them," said the guard as he noticed Betsy's nervous glance at the horses as she stood ready to board the coach.

"What's a miller?" she asked her father.

"It's a horse given to kicking. Luckily it seems we haven't one for the first stage of this journey," replied her father.

The guard, with his blunderbuses and two pistols, looked well able to defend them. He would be travelling to Newmarket where a new guard would take over. The first guard then travelled back to Norwich on another coach. Guards were needed for there were sometimes thieves waiting in remote areas to attack and rob the travellers on the bad roads.

Once everyone was settled inside the coach and five well wrapped up passengers were sitting on the roof, the guard sounded his horn and they were on their way. With the four straining horses whipped up to a full gallop, the coach swinging and creaking at speed, the passengers must have been only too aware that accidents were common. Betsy talked to her father and a lady companion but still found the journey a strain.

Just past Newmarket, they reached a small inn

and the coach stopped for a time. This was fortunate for Betsy who had toothache. Her father was able to buy something at the inn to ease the pain. This with a small drink of brandy soothed her nerves and helped her to go to sleep during the next stage of the journey.

On reaching London they went to Brick Lane to stay with some relatives. The next day Joseph Gurney had left London on business. When after a few days, her relatives also had to leave, Betsy found herself virtually alone in London to do as she wished. Fortunately her diary has supplied the details of how she spent her time. She decided to see the sights of the city and visit all the most famous theatres.

Her first choice on Monday evening was Drury Lane Theatre where there were always good actors and large audiences. The theatre was lit by candles which were also on each side of the stage and gave a wonderful effect but were a fire danger. The seats were hard benches and the audience could get increasingly uncomfortable and noisy. Betsy noted in her diary that she found the theatre to be a grand place but she was disappointed with the plays. On the next day she went to Covent Garden Theatre, then a forty-six year old building, doomed to be burned down twenty years later.

Betsy did not enjoy her visit to Covent Garden Theatre and felt on Wednesday evening that she would like to do something different. So she went for a dancing lesson. On the next evening she was still seeking entertainment. Many theatres offered a variety of items for the evening's programme. There could be a comedy, ballet and a play, all in the same evening. Betsy found a theatre with Hamlet and Bluebeard on the same programme. She decided to go and although she made no comment about Hamlet, she seemed to have enjoyed the music and scenery of Bluebeard.

These theatre visits were not especially enjoyed by Betsy. It was all new and she had no friends to share the experience. By Friday she was feeling homesick and would have welcomed the chance to go back to Earlham and see her sisters. The capital city could be an unfriendly place compared with the familiar buildings and people she knew in Norwich.

The houses of London seemed to continue endlessly in all directions and there were barbaric entertainments that attracted large crowds but Betsy would never see. Typical of these were cock-fighting at the New Red Lion Cockpit at Clerkenwell, bear-baiting with dogs at the Bear Garden, Hockley-in-the-Hole and boxing without boxing gloves.

When her relatives returned to Brick Lane, Betsy went with them to more theatres and to art galleries. Each day there was always something new to see and do. Some friends, the Opies, took her to the opera. She saw a performance also attended by the Prince of Wales, the future King George IV. Betsy was so excited to see the Prince that she could not think about the singing and music.

William Savery was also in London and Betsy met him again and went to his Meetings. Every time she heard him speak it made her think more deeply about religion and the life that she was leading. There were distractions too from religious thoughts. This stay in London was crammed with visits and many pleasures.

One such visit was to her relatives in Hampstead, the Hoare family. They were wealthy people who loved having Betsy to stay with them. They wanted her to enjoy herself, so they took her again to the opera. She wrote to her sisters in Norwich, telling them about the wonderful time she was having and how kind everyone was. But she couldn't resist writing to her sisters with a special reminder that they should be good and kind to each other.

After nearly two months in London, Betsy began to feel homesick again. She had been to most of the exciting places, met lots of interesting people and enjoyed her freedom in a way that she had never done before. She had dressed in fine clothes, danced and been to parties. Now she felt a little weary of it all and found herself missing her family and friends in Norwich. She was pleased to see her father when he returned to London in April and to go back home with him.

Back at Earlham Hall, she had much to tell her sisters and was happy to see them all again. They were still the same family of happy girls, enjoying their dancing, singing and riding. Betsy believed that she should do more than just enjoy pleasures. She went to Meeting in Norwich every

Sunday and did not always join her sisters for their dancing and singing. She would sometimes go off on her own which made her sisters think she was unfriendly.

One day she went into the park and noticed a girl of about her own age sitting there with a large bag. The two girls started to talk and the girl with the bag said her name was Molly Norman. She looked very poor and Betsy felt sorry for her.

"I can't afford new clothing but at least I have flour in this bag that I can bake," said Molly.

"How much would you need to buy clothes for this year?" Betsy asked.

"About ten shillings I should think."

It was a lot of money for a poor girl like Molly but not for the Gurney family. Betsy went home and spoke to her father.

"Today I met a girl who can't afford to buy herself clothing," she said. "She's a good, hard-working girl who deserves to be better treated. From my allowance of forty pounds a year, I could give her the ten shillings she needs for clothing."

"If you'd like to do this for the girl then certainly you may do it," said Mr Gurney.

Betsy was delighted and when she saw Molly again she gave her the money she needed. She saw Molly regularly, teaching her about the Bible and eventually engaging her as a family servant. For her own part, Betsy was thinking more and more about the meaning of religion and every morning she read a passage from the Bible before she had her breakfast.

In the Summer of 1798 John Gurney took his family on a journey that went through south-west England and into Wales. It was during this journey that Betsy met Deborah Darby, a famous Quaker preacher. The Gurneys were staying at the house of Richard Reynolds, a Quaker. Betsy's cousin, Priscilla Hannah Gurney, also lived in the house. Priscilla was a Quaker Minister and in her simple clothing, impressed Betsy with her sincerity. Together Priscilla and Betsy walked around Coalbrookdale, the centre for the iron works, owned by a famous Quaker family, the Darbys.

One morning Deborah Darby, a friend of Priscilla, came to breakfast and met Betsy. It was one of the most important meetings in Betsy's life for Deborah spoke in such a clear and under-standing way that she seemed to solve many of Betsy's problems. Betsy was very excited and looked forward to their next meeting a few days later.

This time Betsy, Priscilla and Richard Reynolds visited Deborah Darby's home and again Betsy was inspired when Deborah spoke.

"You will have unusual power to help others in your life," said Deborah. "I believe you will bring light to the blind, speech to the dumb and feet to the lame."

As Deborah talked to her, Betsy felt strongly that she would like to be able to give up her easy life and do something really worthwhile for others less fortunate than herself. She also felt a strong urge to put away her showy, expensive clothing and wear simple dark dresses and bonnets like a true Quaker woman. Betsy never forgot Deborah's words which had a lasting effect on her thinking. But she was still only eighteen and it was difficult to make any immediate changes in her life.

When she returned to Earlham she was soon involved in the daily routine of studying French, needlework, walking in the park and enjoying dances and parties. For these she had to wear fine clothes and join in the fun with the others. She thought about the poor however, helped Molly Norman and encouraged poor local women to bring their small children to her Sunday school in Earlham. She had discovered a seldom used laundry at the back of the house. Betsy believed this would make an ideal classroom and asked her father if she could use it. John Gurney was not happy about some of Betsy's ideas but he was a kindly man and agreed to let her do as she wished.

A crowd of children from poor homes were soon tramping into Earlham Hall. Her sisters laughed at first but when their numbers grew to about seventy children, they were not so amused.

"These children spoil our home," said Louisa one Sunday morning when she found herself surrounded by what were now known as Betsy's young 'imps'.

"Don't be jealous of these young ones," said Betsy. "Apart from the little learning I give them, they have nothing while we have everything."

At other times her sisters teased Betsy because her own writing and spelling were poor and yet she was teaching others. They knew too that she had never been able to do needlework but now was struggling to teach sewing to the girls. In spite of all her difficulties Betsy managed to keep the children happy, especially when she read stories to them from the Bible. She was now using money of her own to buy books for the school as well as helping Molly Norman to buy clothes.

Her father was aware of the attitude of his other daughters towards Betsy's Sunday school and he was not pleased about her spending money on it. There was a growing number of parents who wanted their children to attend the school, which had become quite a large concern.

"The money I give you is for your own needs," her father told her. "Your school's getting too big and buying books for all the children is a waste of money."

"I sometimes visit their homes," said Betsy. "Many of these people suffer terrible poverty and their children have a great need for books."

"You know I help the poor whenever I can," said her father. "But you can't disturb your family in this way and in any case it makes you late for your Sunday dinner." Betsy tried to avoid an argument but she did not close down the school.

She was at that time becoming increasingly interested in the work of the Society of Friends. In March 1799 she was in London with her sister

Rachel. They had both been invited to a party by their London cousins. When they were getting ready to go, Rachel found her sister trying on a Quaker cap.

"Don't worry, I haven't made my mind up to wear it," said Betsy, self-consciously removing the cap.

"I have no complaint about it," replied Rachel. "If you want to wear it, I should do so."

In the end Betsy wore her Quaker cap to the party.

It was the fashion of the time to keep a diary and Betsy and her sisters were no exceptions. Their brother, John Gurney, had a friend named Joseph Fry, a young banker with a hearty, friendly manner, but a loud laugh that irritated most of the Gurney sisters. Joseph liked Betsy and came as often as he could to see her. On 25 July 1799 she wrote in her diary that she believed he wanted to marry her.

On the next day Joseph proposed to her. She knew her family did not think he would make a suitable husband. Joseph had to wait for a day, only to learn that she had turned him down. At that time Betsy was occupying her spare moments studying long books on English and history. She also became increasingly active in the Quaker movement.

On 12 December Joseph wrote to say that he would like to visit Earlham Hall again. Betsy was secretly pleased and stopped her father writing to Joseph to put off the visit. In the end he came as he had requested as a guest but again left without

Betsy agreeing to their marriage. Joseph Fry was shy and awkward and although Betsy liked him, she felt a strong need to be independent. It looked as if it would take a long time for her to make up her mind. Then one day Joseph tried a different approach.

"I want you to accept this gift from me," he told her.

They were standing in the gardens of Earlham Hall and Betsy could see her sisters hiding behind some laurel bushes and watching her. She picked up the gift from the garden seat where Joseph had placed it and saw that it was a fine gold watch with a chain.

"Thank you, Joseph," she said. "It's beautiful."

"There is a condition," continued Joseph. "If you don't wish to marry me, return the watch to me by nine o'clock in the morning and I'll leave Earlham Hall for the last time."

Betsy did not return the watch. And so they began preparations for the marriage. There was much to do. For instance for some time Betsy had been in the habit of visiting the local poor, taking them food and clothing. She knew that once married she would not be able to continue this work and so she made a special effort to collect as much clothing as possible for what would be her last visits to the poor people living in the cottages around Earlham.

Then there were her 'imps'. She certainly could not forget about them for there were eighty-six of them by then, all well-behaved, if tatty, little urchins. Betsy loved her time with them on Sunday when she could hold their attention with her stories and she knew she would greatly miss them, as they would miss her.

She had been so determined to wear the plain clothes of Quakers that her sisters began to make fun of her when they saw the expensive things their father was buying for her wedding trousseau.

"What a fine trousseau you have," said Kitty, perhaps jealous of her sister's coming wedding. "I'm surprised it doesn't offend your Quaker beliefs."

"This is my special day," replied Betsy. "It doesn't trouble me as I have not had silken clothing for a long time."

Her other sisters also said unkind things about Joseph, calling him "young Fry" and making fun of his clumsy manners. Betsy tried not to take any notice of them and busied herself with her Quaker Meetings and her plans for the wedding. The Fry family, wealthy Quakers in the City of London, now came to Earlham Hall to discuss the wedding arrangements.

The wedding was to take place at the Meeting House in Goats Lane and immediately afterwards Joseph and Betsy were to stay at the holiday home of her Uncle Richard at Hempstead in Norfolk. Joseph's parents lived in a large country mansion in Plashet, Essex, and he was invited to bring Betsy here to stay until they moved to a permanent home in London.

On Sunday 12 August 1800 the eighty-six poor

children who had attended her Sunday school came to say goodbye. Both Betsy and many of the children were in tears and Betsy knew she would have to make her home in London even though she liked living near Norwich.

The wedding took place on Sunday 19 August before a large crowd of relatives and friends. It was an emotional moment as well as a happy one and Betsy could not hide her tears during the ceremony. She was the first of the Gurney sisters to marry. Her father too, was saddened to lose his daughter.

For Betsy it was the beginning of a new chapter in her life. She was now Mrs Elizabeth Fry and was called Elizabeth from the time of her marriage. At the age of twenty she was now to be the mistress of a large house with many servants and guests.

3

MILDRED'S COURT

"I THINK I'll go for a walk in the gardens," said Elizabeth, looking through the window at the display of flowers under the trees. "I've a slight headache and the fresh air will do me good."

Her mother-in-law, Mother Fry as Joseph called her, looked carefully at Elizabeth in a way that was irritating, as if she was examining her face for signs of strain.

"You look a little pale," she said. "Why don't you have a rest before tea. I think it's all those books you read. They trouble your eyes."

Elizabeth Fry had been at Plashet for a month and already she was bored and longing to go back and see Earlham Hall again. It was not that Mother Fry was unfriendly but she was always fussing about Elizabeth resting and telling her how it was necessary to eat lots of good food.

"No I'm quite all right thank you," said Elizabeth and she got up and left the room to wander into the gardens.

"What a strange girl she is," said Mother Fry to her daughter. "She just doesn't seem to be able to enjoy a nice little gossip."

"If you ask me," said her daughter, "she's just too high and mighty."

Elizabeth had always been regarded as the odd one out at Earlham Hall because she was too serious. She now found that although she had married Joseph Fry she was still different from her in-laws. As far as they were concerned she was not sufficiently a Quaker. She was not the plain, simple girl that they felt Joseph should have married. Elizabeth on the other hand found them rather narrow minded and a little rough mannered.

The Fry family owned a warehouse in London next to a building called Mildred's Court. This was where Joseph and Elizabeth Fry were going to live. As the house was not yet ready for them, in October Elizabeth arranged to leave Plashet for a while and pay a visit to Earlham Hall. She wrote in her diary, "I never was so glad at the thought of seeing any place."

In November Joseph and Elizabeth moved to London. She found Mildred's Court a shock after the life she had been leading. Tea, coffee and spices were stored in the warehouse. There was a counting house on the ground floor and lodgings for a number of clerks. The servants had just lost their old mistress, Eliza Fry, Elizabeth's sister-in-law, and they did not take too kindly to the new young mistress who had arrived.

From early in the morning until late in the evening Elizabeth found herself fully occupied with running Mildred's Court. On the day she arrived she was surprised to receive a visit for dinner from William Fry, her husband's brother but this was only the beginning. Any member of the Fry family who arrived in London felt it their right to receive hospitality at Mildred's Court. So Elizabeth had a never ending stream of relatives expecting food and lodging for as long as they wished.

Not far from Mildred's Court were two Quaker Meeting Houses. Any Quaker who came to London and knew the Frys, and most of them did, came to visit Mildred's Court. They expected hospitality and were given it but the burden fell upon Elizabeth who had to make all the arrangements to see that she had enough food and beds for them. Sometimes they held long meetings in her home, making Elizabeth so bored and weary, that she wondered how she could have chosen such a life. At least at Earlham Hall she had felt she was helping her imps and some of the local poor people.

In spite of having so much to do now that she was married, Elizabeth Fry did not forget about the people in London who were so much poorer and less fortunate than herself. She started to walk through the streets near her home to see how people were living, and what a terrible shock she had. There were rows of hovels where the walls were falling down and the floors were rotten with damp and filth. In one alley she told some boys to stop throwing stones or they would break the windows.

"What windows?" shouted one of the urchins. "There are no windows."

When Elizabeth looked along the row of houses she saw that the boy was right. Hardly any house had proper windows. Some of them had been left as empty holes so that the rain and wind could blow in unchecked. Others had been stuffed up with pieces of grimy rag. There was nothing Elizabeth could do about these slum houses but she could do a little to help the people and their children.

She got to know them so that they would talk to her and tell her about their problems. Winter was an especially difficult time for them as their threadbare clothes did not keep them warm. Food too was always a desperate need and the only way some of them could keep alive was by stealing. If they were caught they could receive terrible punishments.

"You mustn't go out alone," said Joseph when his wife came back from one of her London walks. "It's far too dangerous for a woman to walk in such streets."

"There are many women trying to live in houses on those streets," replied Elizabeth. "Many of them are starving. We must do something to help. It's not right that no one should care."

"Is it really as bad as you say?" asked Joseph. "Perhaps they're just dishonest people who would rather steal than work."

"I'm sure that's not so," said Elizabeth. "I've talked to these people and feel I am already getting to know them. Why don't you come with me and see for yourself how they have to live."

So Joseph, after some doubt, went with Elizabeth to explore the narrow streets and alleys not far from Mildred's Court. There were no proper drains and sewers and the broken down hovels contained many people ill with fever. Everywhere they saw poverty that Joseph had never realised existed. They saw one small boy sitting on a stone step by a door. He was thin, pale and shivering with cold.

"Is that your home?" asked Joseph.

"Nah! I ain't got a home," replied the boy.

Shocked, Joseph Fry questioned the boy further and discovered that he had neither a home nor parents. It seemed terrible that this small child had nowhere to live except the shelter of doorways and no one to care for him. He managed to live by stealing either money or food. Joseph found a coin and gave it to the boy who ran off in delight, hardly believing his luck.

"There are many such boys," said Elizabeth. "Most of them are taught to steal by old thieves."

Before they reached home they saw other children sitting in the gutters. There was a slight chance of help from charities run by a few kindly people but most of these children were left to fend for themselves. Joseph and Elizabeth noticed two boys handing over some watches and other items to a man in a doorway.

"They've spent their day as pickpockets," said Elizabeth. "They work for the man who takes everything they have stolen."

Joseph had taken Elizabeth to the beautiful shops of Pall Mall, which were said to be the finest shops not only in London but also in the whole of Europe. All kinds of goods were on display but they were very expensive and only a few wealthy people such as Joseph could afford to buy them. Now Joseph had to agree with Elizabeth that they were indeed rich while others were too poor to buy clothes to wear and food to eat.

Quakers were among the few charity workers who tried to help the poor in London. They had started a small school in Islington and asked Elizabeth if she could help there. Although she had run her Sunday school at home in Norwich, she was nervous at first about taking on this work. However, she tried reading her Bible stories to the children in her quiet, friendly voice and found that they loved to listen.

By the autumn of 1803 Elizabeth and Joseph had two children of their own, Katherine and Rachel, but this did not stop Elizabeth working for the poor. About this time she was in a street near her home when a woman came up to her begging for help. She looked so weary and poor that Elizabeth wanted to help to do something to make this woman's life better. So she went back to the same street, hoping to see the woman and give her money. But the streets were full of people and noise as the tradesmen shouted out the things they had for sale.

For hours Elizabeth walked among the crowds, looking all the time for the beggar woman, but she could not find her. On her way home, though, she noticed two other women who were very poor. She started to talk to them, asking them about their families and how they lived.

"I have not eaten today," said one. "I've only enough money to buy a little food for my children."

"You're lucky," said the other. "My family can only eat when we steal. One day we'll be caught and sent to prison."

"I'm your friend," said Elizabeth. "And I would like to help you. Take this money and buy the things you need."

The two women were very grateful and thanked Elizabeth again and again before they left her. They told their friends of the young, well dressed woman who was so kind to them. Soon the bell at the door of Mildred's Court was always ringing as the message spread among the local poor that the lady at that house was generous to those in need.

Elizabeth now always wore her Quaker cap with a plain dress of dull colours. She remained active as a Quaker, going to Meeting, helping the poor and attending to her school. At the same time her own family increased year by year. She was eventually to have ten children, many of them named after her family at Norwich. There was Katherine, Rachel, John, William, Rich enda, Joseph, Elizabeth, Hannah, Louisa, Samuel and Daniel. Elizabeth, her namesake, became ill and died at the age of four.

Winter was always a hard time for the poor of London. There were so many neglected children that it made Elizabeth desperate to help them. One especially cold winter she was especially touched by a tragic story. A small boy had been so frozen in the cold that he had died. Elizabeth appealed to other Quaker ladies for help. Food, clothing and medical help were urgently needed. The ladies responded at once by offering money to pay for the food. Elizabeth set up a centre in an old barn where the ladies helped to serve soup and supply clothing to the many poor people that came there.

Some of the people that came for help were not only hungry but also very ill. Elizabeth was a good nurse and bandaged their injuries and supplied them with medicines, all paid for by herself and her Quaker ladies. London, with more than half a million people, had so many poor that it seemed Elizabeth's attempts to provide help for them could never completely succeed.

Apart from her work with the poor people of London, Elizabeth was spending much of her time away from home. She had discovered that she had great powers as a speaker and she visited Quaker Meeting places all over Britain. She always held the interest of large audiences as she explained to them her beliefs of what religion really meant to her.

Joseph Fry was a kind and considerate husband who helped Elizabeth as much as he could. He was willing at times to stay at home and care for the children while she was away. At other times she would go back to Earlham Hall and leave her children there to be looked after by her sisters who were still living there. Molly Norman was still working as a nanny and loved to care for Elizabeth's young children. Other relatives also helped to care for them when Elizabeth went on her journeys. The children were lively and not well behaved and caused difficulties when they had to be away from home.

"It's time Elizabeth stayed at home and looked after her own unruly children," was a typical comment of the various aunts who had to mind them. In her heart Elizabeth knew this was true but she also was aware that she had a mission in the world to make life better for others and nothing, not even her family, could come before that.

In May 1807 she returned to Earlham Hall for the wedding of her young sister Hannah to Fowell Buxton, a Quaker who later became a Member of Parliament, speaking against slavery and getting the support of Elizabeth. This was a happy time for her.

In 1808, when Elizabeth had five children, her husband engaged a governess to look after and teach the children at Mildred's Court. Elizabeth had met a young Quaker named Joseph Lancaster who was pioneering new methods of education to help poor children. He divided his boys into groups of twelve with a monitor to take each group and report to the teacher. This way one teacher could handle a large number of boys and still get good results. These ideas impressed Elizabeth and she used them in her own schools.

That same year Joseph Fry's father died and Joseph inherited the family estate at Plashet in Essex. This was a large house with beautiful grounds and much more suitable for Elizabeth's large family than Mildred's Court in London.

The move to Plashet came in the spring of 1809. Elizabeth had done much for the poor people in London but her work there was not finished. She had made discoveries about the needs of these people that she would never forget. In addition she had travelled the country and seen for herself that it was not only in London that poverty caused terrible suffering.

Elizabeth looked forward to going to live at Plashet. For nine years she had endured the noise and dirt of London. She had never liked Mildred's Court with the constant coming and going of visitors and the busy counting house with the clerks and tradesmen. Running a mansion the size of Plashet would be a new experience but she had been brought up on her parents' estate in Norwich and was not worried by the challenge that the move would bring.

4

A NEW LIFE IN PLASHET

"COME on children. We're going to gather some primroses," said Elizabeth.

Nurse Barns had just brought Katherine and Rachel and their young brother John into the room. She knew what to expect and the three children were dressed ready for a walk to the woods. Outside they were joined by Denis Regan, the gardener, who came along to advise them and help where necessary.

Elizabeth found it was a lovely change from London, to be able to wander in the woods with her children, showing them flowers and other details of nature that caught her eye. The children loved it too, which gave Elizabeth added pleasure. Today they were looking for primroses and a brief search soon brought results.

"Here are some," called Katherine who had wandered a little ahead of the rest and found some small yellow flowers.

Denis Regan agreed that she was right and the children set to work with their trowels digging up some of the plants. When they had gathered a fair number, their mother stopped them.

"Let's continue our search," she said. "We must leave enough here to grow well as it is wrong to spoil the beauty of the woods."

So they moved to another part of the woods and shouts of delight were heard whenever they made a new discovery.

When Elizabeth thought the children had enough primroses, she took them back to the gardens and Denis Regan showed them the flower beds where it would be best to put the new plants. Once again the children were busy with their trowels until all the primroses had been planted. Then they went indoors with Nurse Barns to be washed and have a change of clothing.

Elizabeth was a great believer in reading the Bible. She read it herself whenever she had the time and she read it to her children so that they grew up aware of the Bible's message. The servants at Plashet also had to attend and listen to her regular Bible readings.

On 26 September 1809 an express coach arrived at Plashet bringing her sister Richenda. She brought sad news that their father was very ill at Earlham Hall and was not expected to live. After a long and tiring ride, they arrived at Earlham Hall by midnight. Elizabeth was thankful to find her father still alive.

During the night she sat by her father's bed and talked to him. For long periods he slept but when he woke he talked to her about his life and his family. He told her that the love of his children had always been a great encouragement to him. He was glad his children had high values in their lives and he hoped they would never give way to the temptation to lead any other than a good life.

The following morning John Gurney died. He was fifty-nine years old. Elizabeth was saddened, but her father's words had a great effect upon her. More than ever she was determined that she would make her life worth while and would never stop her efforts, no matter what others might say.

There was within Elizabeth a force that made her act impulsively but with a great sense of purpose. At her father's funeral she was walking with her family to the graveyard when she suddenly knelt down and said a prayer. Her family were embarrassed but Elizabeth rose and continued to walk quietly with them. She had for a long time wanted to preach at Quaker meetings. From this time onwards, she always did so.

It was very unusual for a woman who lived at the beginning of the 19th century to make her own decisions in this way. It was obvious, not only to Elizabeth herself but also to those who knew her, that she was a very unusual woman with a determination that overcame all obstacles.

One day in September 1811 Elizabeth visited Earlham Hall to attend a meeting of the British and Foreign Bible Society in Norwich which was to be addressed by the Bishop of Norwich. Afterwards, her brother Joseph Gurney invited thirty-four members of the Society to dinner at Earlham. It was all very grand as they sat down to dine in the large dining-hall. It was also unusual for there were Quakers dining with Church of

England clergymen, Baptists and others.

"Will you please ask for silence?" Elizabeth said to Richard Phillips, a Quaker whom she knew. It was the end of the meal and Richard was not sure what was going to happen but he did as Elizabeth had asked and all voices stilled and a great hush came over the hall.

To the astonishment of the gathering, Elizabeth knelt before them and started to pray to God for his blessing. She then continued a long sermon on the importance of religion and truth on earth. She spoke in such a manner that the attention of all the guests was completely held. Many of them felt that they had gone through a very special religious experience after they had listened to Elizabeth.

When she finished her audience drank their wine and discussed what had happened. She had spoken to them like a person inspired by the word of God and they were very impressed. Yet it was most strange to them that it had been a woman who had preached in this way. Not all of them approved, including her own brothers and sisters. John and Daniel especially thought that it was wrong for women to want to preach.

It was certainly true that Elizabeth's constant travels caused something of a burden to others. When she went to Earlham Hall she often left her children there while she went off to a Quaker Meeting. At first they had been welcomed but as they grew older her children became noisy and rude. Her sister Louisa did not like their untidiness and became angry at any signs of rudeness.

"Have we got to have those brats again?" she would say when Elizabeth turned up with them.

Elizabeth would sit with her children whenever she had the time, read to them from the Bible, teach them prayers and hymns and try to reassure them that although she was often away, they were always in her thoughts. She was hurt when she realised her sisters thought that she sometimes neglected her children.

By the year 1812 when Elizabeth was thirty-two years of age, she had a family of eight children. It was not a good year for either business or the condition of the people in the country. The war against Napoleon had caused a great decline in trade and Joseph's business prospects were bad. Many people could not find work, goods were in short supply and prices were going up. Elizabeth was aware that many villagers who lived near Plashet were struggling to make a living.

As usual she tried to organise help for them by giving them food and clothing. This she did by appealing to local Quaker ladies to work with her in providing relief for the poor. Elizabeth's reputation soon spread among the local poor as a lady to whom they could always look for help.

She was worried also about the education of the children and set up a school for some of the girls in the district. She had never forgotten the methods used by Joseph Lancaster when she met him years before. Now that she had her own girls' school she used Lancaster's ideas.

The school was one room in a house close to

Plashet. Elizabeth paid a teacher, though visited the school herself to read to the girls and to look at their work. Girls who pleased her with good work were awarded prizes of Bibles.

Joseph Fry's tea business was losing money as were so many other businesses at that time. Living at Plashet was expensive and in an effort to save money they decided to move back to Mildred's Court for the winter. Everyone was feeling the effect of poor trade and rising costs. The factory system was getting under way which meant that people who had worked as craftsmen at home found themselves out of work. Some who came to the cities might find work in a factory but hours were long, conditions bad and wages very low.

So when Joseph and Elizabeth returned with their family to London, they found terrible living conditions for the poor around Mildred's Court and much discontent. Even bread was very expensive and the anger of the poor was shown when they attacked better off people in the street. The king received some blame, and the crowds jeered at his coach and tried to throw mud and stones at it.

While they were living at Plashet Elizabeth Fry had made it her concern to visit the poor people living in the cottages near her home. She took them soup and extra material for clothing. She got to know them and made friends with them. She knew how urgently the genuine poor needed warmth and food.

In London the poverty of thousands of people

was obvious for all to see. It was impossible for Elizabeth to know them all. Many of them too had turned to crime such as burglary and pocket picking to make a living. Those caught were cruelly punished by harsh prison sentences, flogging, being deported or put to death by execution. Women caught breaking the law were just as severely punished as the men.

One cold day in January 1813 Elizabeth had a visit from a French-American Quaker named Stephen Grellet. He was a wealthy French aristocrat who had settled in the United States where he joined the Society of Friends. He had already seen much suffering among the poor of the United States and France.

Now that he was in England he was concerned about the crime that went on in London. He let it be known that he would be attending the Meeting House in St Martin's Lane to help people who had been forced to become criminals to make a living. Stephen Grellet had hoped that a number of such people would come to listen to him.

At seven o'clock in the evening he was amazed to find the hall packed with a large crowd, mostly young people. Stephen spoke to them and said prayers for them. They promised to lead better lives and to remember what he had told them about the good effect of religion.

News of this great meeting of pickpockets and thieves and how they had listened with such attention and enthusiasm to Stephen Grellet, the Quaker preacher, spread throughout London.

The Chief Magistrate came to see Grellet and thanked him for what he had done.

"If I gather all the criminals that I can find in London and persuade them to assemble together, will you talk to them and try to make them lead better lives?"

"I would like to see what happens to these people when they are sent to prison," said Grellet. "Could I therefore have permission to visit the prisons?"

This permission was granted and after visiting a number of prisons, Stephen Grellet went to the grim buildings of Newgate where criminals were still hanged in public. He was horrified to find many young boys in the prison, mixing with men criminals.

"These boys will never have a chance to grow into honest citizens," said Grellet to the friend who had gone with him. "We must make sure that in future they are not allowed to be together in this way."

When Grellet went to the rooms in the prison yard where the women prisoners lived, he was stopped by the gaoler.

"It would be unsafe to go in there."

"I understand these prisoners are women," said Grellet. "Why should it be unsafe for visitors?"

"You forget that many of them are desperate and therefore dangerous. We have to be careful with them," the gaoler insisted.

Grellet and his friend would not be put off and entered the rooms occupied by the women. He was shocked by the dirt and general conditions he saw. Most of the women were in hammocks but many slept on dirty straw on the floor. The filthy state of the rooms and the women's clothing horrified the two visitors. The women were surprised to see two men appear suddenly and started to ask them questions, but there was no trouble.

"There are more prisoners upstairs," one woman told them.

So Grellet and his friend went upstairs where they found women who were ill. They were deeply shocked at the sight of so many pale, sick-looking women lying either on the hard stone floor or on bits of dirty straw. Grellet was especially concerned that some of these women, clothed in tatty, dirty clothes, sat with small babies in their arms.

Stephen Grellet left Newgate Prison, determined that something must be done to help the hundreds of wretched women prisoners he had seen. He remembered his friend Elizabeth Fry. He knew she was living at Mildred's Court in London and that she had already achieved a reputation as a worker for the poor. He decided to go to her and ask for her advice and help.

"I know you are aware of the desperate situation of the poor people of this city. There are bad criminals among them, no doubt, but many of them would starve if they did not steal," Grellet told her.

"Everywhere I try to read to these people the words of the Bible, so they'll attempt to lead a better life," said Elizabeth. "But what one person can do alone is not enough."

"I have come from Newgate Prison where women are living in worse conditions than animals in cages," said Grellet. "They know nothing of the Bible and exist without hope. Their clothes are filthy and tattered and they sleep amidst dirt and squalor. What is worse, they have babies and young children with them."

"Do you mean that no one is concerned for these children?" Elizabeth asked, immediately feeling concern herself.

"They are not," said Grellet. "I saw many babies without warm clothing. They were crying because of the cold and some of them were ill."

"Isn't the prison Governor interested in the fate of these women and children?"

"He's too scared to go near them and doesn't want to know about them," said Grellet. "They are women and children without hope."

"Then they must be given hope. I will go to this Governor and make him care about the human beings that have to be in this dreadful place," said Elizabeth. "I know my sister-in-law, Anna Buxton, will help. We will go to Newgate, take clothes to the women and talk to them."

"I'm afraid that may not be possible," he said. "I had great difficulty getting permission to visit the women's rooms in Newgate myself."

Elizabeth was haunted by Grellet's account of the terrible situation in Newgate. She contacted Anna Buxton, who at once agreed to come with her to the prison. Then she asked some Quaker girls to make as many simple, warm dresses as they could. Elizabeth bought the material, the girls set to work and before the next day was over she had bundles of clothes for the children in the prison. Accompanied by Anna, Elizabeth set off, carrying the clothing and a Bible.

Of the eighteen prisons in London at that time, Newgate was believed to be the worst. It was unknown for any lady to visit such a place. That did not worry Elizabeth. She entered the grey and forbidding prison gates and asked to see the Governor.

"I wish to be taken to see the women of this prison," she told him.

He was horrified at the idea and sat looking at the two ladies before him in sheer disbelief.

"I don't think you realise the risks you take if you go in there," he said. "Even my turnkeys go in as little as possible and then never alone."

"Thank you for your warning, but we are not afraid," said Elizabeth.

"They will see that you are ladies and might make a savage attack on you," the Governor continued. "I cannot allow you to risk injury and even death."

"Please let us go in. Don't concern yourself for our welfare but for the condition of these poor women and their children," she insisted.

Elizabeth agreed to leave behind her watch in case it was stolen. At last the Governor allowed the turnkeys to open the great prison doors. Then Elizabeth and Anna were taken to the women's quarters. As they went into the yard some of the women saw them and pushed their skinny arms through the bars screaming for money. The women at the back, hearing that there were visitors, tried to push to the front and get their own hands through the bars. It was a horrible scene as the women screamed and fought each other, and frightening for the visitors. Elizabeth stopped to speak, explaining to the women that she was there to help them.

The turnkey led them to the so-called infirmary where sick women and their children were lying on the hard floor without either warmth or comfort. The women and children, who were dirty and shivering with cold, stared at Elizabeth and Anna.

"What do these women and their children have to eat and drink?" Elizabeth asked the turnkey.

"A piece of bread and some water," he replied.

"That's all they have day after day?"

The turnkey nodded and Elizabeth turned away to touch the children and speak to the women. She could see that many of the children were so ill that they would never recover. As Elizabeth talked in her kind, gentle voice, the women gathered around her to listen. She told them that she too was a mother and then she picked up one of the small children and held it close to her.

"I have something nice and warm for you," she said.

Then with Anna she set to work distributing all the bundles of clothing that they had brought for the babies and children. Then she turned to the turnkey.

"Will you see that all this dirty straw is taken away and replaced with clean," she said.

The turnkey, nervous that at any moment both he and the visitors would be attacked, willingly agreed that clean straw would be fetched but did not need to fear for their safety. Elizabeth spoke to the women in a friendly, quiet manner. She tried to encourage and give them hope and they found themselves losing their suspicions and began to regard her as a friend.

When all the clothing had been shared out and the clean straw had replaced the old, Elizabeth spoke to the women again. She explained that she wanted to help them but they also must try to improve themselves. Before she left, she promised she would come back and see them again soon.

How fortunate she felt she and Anna were to be able to walk free from Newgate Prison while hundreds of women were confined there, often for some quite trivial offence. The memory of the dirt, smell and despair of the prison made her shudder at the thought of going back. Her own clothing had been stained by the stench of dirty prison air and once back at Mildred's Court, she had a bath and changed into a clean dress.

True to her word, Elizabeth made immediate plans for her next Newgate visit. This time she arranged for her friends to collect clothing for the women and also to make as much soup as it would be possible to take to the prison. She had not been satisfied with the supply of new straw for the women's bedding and so she also had taken to the prison a quantity of thick, clean straw.

With these supplies, she returned to Newgate and again managed to be shown to the women's prison quarters. She shared out the clothing and made sure that everyone had a bowl of hot soup. She promised the women she would never forget them and would do everything possible to make their lives better. When she left, many of the women prisoners wept to see her go.

5

THE HEROINE OF NEWGATE

"THESE people must be made warm or they will die," said Elizabeth.

"Yes, of course they need help in this cold weather, but remember you too will soon have another baby and I think you tire yourself too much."

Elizabeth had just returned from a meeting with her ladies who had agreed to make large quantities of broth to give to the local poor. On arriving home, she had found her husband waiting for her. He had been about to complain to his wife about the continual callers at their home begging for food and clothing. He was also annoyed that the children from the nearby district of Bow came into the grounds of their home to play and beg. When he saw how weary his wife looked, however, Joseph could not bring himself to grumble too much.

After their stay in London and Elizabeth's visits to Newgate, they returned to their estate at Plashet. The winter of early 1814 was very cold and crops were poor. Elizabeth had soon organised help for the poor and was constantly at work, distributing hot broth and clothing. She had so much to do she made herself tired and ill. In addition to her work with the poor, there was the school which she had opened. Although it was run by a teacher, Elizabeth was a frequent visitor, giving Bible readings and general encouragement to the girls.

She also liked to wander round the cottages and the nearby gypsy camp. She would talk to these people, listen to their stories and sometimes give them Bibles. They were also likely to receive advice on how to look after their children.

Elizabeth was forced to rest for a time when her ninth baby, Louisa, was born in June that year. This brought joy but there was great sadness later the same year when her four year old daughter Betsy became ill with fever and died.

Joseph Fry's business was not prospering and again they found living at Plashet was too costly. So by January 1815 they were once more back at Mildred's Court and became the poor relations of the Gurney and Fry families. It made little difference to Elizabeth's work though, as throughout 1815 she continued to travel by coach, often with one of her children on long, tiring and dangerous journeys to attend Quaker meetings.

The return of soldiers from the war with France, the lack of work and poverty were some of the reasons for an increase in crime at this time. The government tried to lessen the crime by harsh punishments and deporting criminals to Australia. Elizabeth already knew what was going on in the prisons and had tried to help. Now she turned her attention once more to the welfare of the prisoners in Newgate.

At Christmas time, in 1816, Elizabeth went to Newgate Prison with written permission to meet and talk with the women prisoners. The turnkey had no wish to go among these criminals that he considered dangerous, so it was with reluctance that he unlocked the prison doors. Conditions seemed as terrible as when she had gone there three years before. The women were quarrelling with each other and ragged, ill-looking children were still living in this dreadful place.

The women crowded round her, arguing and cursing but when she spoke they quietened. She sat in her Quaker bonnet and plain clothing and calmly talked to them about what should be done.

"I am a mother with many children and it distresses me to see so many of your children cold and ill this Christmas time. Is there nothing we can do to help them?"

"We have nothing to give them," one of the women cried.

"Their future is hopeless," shouted another.

"You must never give up hope," said Elizabeth. "These children of yours must not grow up to be criminals."

The women listened with tears in their eyes to this quiet thirty-six year old lady. They trusted her and wanted to help but could not see what could be done in such a place as Newgate Prison.

"If I could get permission to start a school for your children here in the prison, would you agree to that?"

"We'd agree to that," shouted one woman and the others joined in the general agreement to the idea.

Encouraged by the attitude of the women, Elizabeth went to the governor of Newgate and the Sheriffs of London. She explained the urgent need for a school in Newgate Prison but found that although her suggestion was listened to with respect, they did not think it would work. When Elizabeth demanded to know why they thought this, they explained that the children would fight each other and damage everything. It would be impossible to teach them.

Elizabeth went away but she promised to be back again and again until they saw her point of view was right. When she returned she was told that there was just no room in the prison for any kind of classroom. So although they were very sorry, they were afraid the idea of a prison school would have to be forgotten.

"So the only problem is that there is no room for a classroom?" Elizabeth asked.

"Yes, that is so," said the governor.

"Then if I could find by some lucky chance, a room in the prison that was empty, I could have it for a classroom?"

"Yes, you could, but as a check has already been made, there is no chance of that," the governor said, assuming that the matter was now over.

He had underestimated the determination of Elizabeth Fry. She returned to Newgate Prison and again talked to the women and explained that she was having difficulties starting a school because there was no room in the prison.

"There is one room that used to be a cell but is now used as a storeroom," said one woman.

Elizabeth was delighted. She went at once to look at the room. It was small but it would make a classroom once it had been cleaned and whitewashed. She wasted no time but hurried to the governor to tell him about the room and remind him of his promise. The governor could see no way out but to let Elizabeth have the room.

"I realise you mean well and you can try your experiment," he said, "but I think with those children it will be hopeless."

The next day Elizabeth was back at Newgate, telling them that they had their school and now she wanted them to choose a teacher. There was a young woman prisoner named Mary O'Connor who was well educated and had been accused wrongly of stealing a watch. She was serving a prison sentence in Newgate. After a vote among the women, Mary was chosen to be the new schoolteacher. The school had thirty children. A few of them were serving prison sentences but mostly they were the children of the women prisoners.

This was a start but Elizabeth was also concerned about the women in the prison. Locked up all day and with nothing useful to do, the women were always in bad moods and quick to quarrel with each other. Elizabeth wanted them to be given useful work. She invited her Quaker lady friends to form the Association for the

Improvement of Female Prisoners in Newgate and the ladies who belonged to her association went to the prison every day to see the prisoners. She also tried to interest others in her plan but they would not help.

Joseph Fry and Elizabeth then invited Governor Newman of Newgate and two other prison officials to their home. Eventually Elizabeth brought up the topic of work for the women to do in prison and said that she would be glad to organise it.

"It's a fine idea but I fear it will not be possible," said the governor. "These women would not favour such a plan."

"If you, Dr Cotton and Mr Bridges will come to a meeting that I can hold with the women next Sunday, you will all be able to see for yourselves."

A meeting like this had never happened before but such was Elizabeth's reputation by now that the three men agreed to be present. So on the following Sunday seventy women prisoners were assembled before the governor and the other officials, Elizabeth Fry, the ladies of her association and the turnkeys.

"We all realise that your time in this prison is not happy," she said. "I would like to suggest that we change the system so that you can have some work to do, a chance to learn and an opportunity to understand religion."

The prisoners, who already looked cleaner and better clad in the clothing that Elizabeth's ladies had brought to the prison, were in full agreement with her ideas. The governor was amazed at both their appearance and their behaviour.

"This new plan is to be tried out, but if we think that you can't behave yourselves and obey the rules, we will stop it at once," he said sternly. "There will be no second chances."

So it was agreed that the Association of Women could visit the prison, appoint a resident matron and arrange useful work for the women to do. It was decided that they could make patchwork quilts which a local firm, Richard Dixon and Company, had agreed to buy. In this way it would be possible for the women to be paid for their work. Eventually this consisted of many different kinds of sewing.

Before they could start work, an empty room was thoroughly cleaned out, whitewashed and made ready as a workroom. Elizabeth explained to the women that when they were in the workshop they would have to observe twelve rules. The women were divided into classes with a monitor chosen from among them and there was a matron to ensure that everything was in order.

"Remember that the monitors will have to check that all rules are being obeyed," she told them. "Now, I'm going to read out the rules one at a time and you will be able to vote on each one of them."

To her great pleasure the women raised their hands to approve every rule. The names of the monitors were then read out and the meeting of prisoners was then closed with a Bible reading and a prayer.

At nine o'clock on 10 April 1818 a bell rang and the women entered for the first opening of their workshop. Dressed in their blue aprons, they looked clean, tidy and were very well behaved. Elizabeth was delighted with the way they worked, and news of her achievement soon spread beyond Newgate. The Lord Mayor of London heard about it.

"Is it possible that Elizabeth Fry could have changed these women?" he asked one day at a meeting of aldermen. When told that there was much talk about the wonderful work of Elizabeth Fry at Newgate, the Mayor was very interested.

"I should like to see for myself," he said. "We must see a typical day in this place."

So arrangements were made for the Mayor and a party of sheriffs and aldermen to visit Newgate. They could hardly believe their eyes when they saw what had happened. Where there had once been a dirty, shouting, fighting rabble without any hope for the future, they found classes of women listening to Bible readings and, in the workroom, more classes busy with their sewing.

Elizabeth Fry was becoming a famous prison reformer. The great improvements that she had brought about in Newgate Prison became known to the government, prison authorities and other reformers. News of her work spread to people all over the country through committees of women prison associations that she set up, and her pioneering reforms were copied by many other prisons.

Elizabeth's reputation meant that she was now constantly meeting many different people. She went to the House of Commons to meet Members of Parliament and to discuss what should be done about prison conditions. Sir Robert Peel, the Home Secretary who was later to become Prime Minister, listened to her views and tried to bring in new laws to improve conditions for women in prison.

She was asked to report on prisons to a House of Commons Committee. Elizabeth wanted better food for the prisoners and better living conditions while she opposed flogging and solitary confinement. Her work was widely reported in the newspapers of that time. But there was still much to do. Many women arrived at Newgate in ragged clothing and Elizabeth tried to give rewards of clothing to those who behaved well in prison. She believed in discipline but through a system of rewards, encouragement and work rather than punishment.

Throughout this period Elizabeth was a minister of the Society of Friends and spoke regularly at Quaker meetings, as well as working so hard for prison reform.

Partly after listening to Elizabeth's suggestions, Robert Peel managed to change some of the criminal laws. Until that time a thief could be convicted and hanged for stealing something worth a few shillings; a poacher could be sent to Australia. Robert Peel greatly reduced the number of crimes that could be punished by hanging. He was also concerned about the totally inadequate system that existed for catching criminals and keeping law and order. So he started a police force with properly trained policemen.

Elizabeth was not always successful in her struggles on behalf of prisoners. In 1818 one girl, Harriett Skelton, had been sentenced to death for forgery. Elizabeth liked Harriett and was very much against the death penalty. She went to see Lord Sidmouth, the Home Secretary after Robert Peel, and when that failed to get a reprieve, she went to ask the help of the Duke of Gloucester. He was sympathetic but could not change the mind of the Home Secretary and the poor girl was hanged.

That same year, Elizabeth became aware of disturbances and riots by some women prisoners in Newgate. She enquired about the trouble and was told by the turnkeys that it was caused by the women's fear of being sent to New South Wales in Australia on a convict ship. She went straight to the women concerned to talk to them. Most of them were in tears and looked desperate.

"I would rather die than go on that hateful ship," said one woman.

"They treat us worse than animals," said another. "We will be put in chains and thrown into waggons before we are taken to the ship."

"No one cares," they shouted.

"Yes, I care and will see that something is done about it," said Elizabeth.

She had found another cause to fight for: human rights for women prisoners sent to Australia.

6

WOMEN AND TRANSPORTATION

"THESE women are the trouble makers," said Governor Newman. "That's why they must be chained and guarded by the turnkeys."

"What happens to them is not justice," Elizabeth insisted as she confronted the Governor in her calm but determined manner.

"They have committed crimes, been found guilty and sentenced to deportation," the Governor explained as he wondered what changes this Quaker lady would want this time.

"I know that you cannot change their sentences but we shouldn't forget that they are human beings. When they leave Newgate they should not be chained and should not be in open waggons where everyone can see them."

"Then what do you suggest?" said the Governor, thinking that there could be no answer, but he was wrong.

"I'll go with them," said Elizabeth. "They must be in hackney-coaches. They can have turnkey guards if you fear they will try to escape but none of them must be chained."

The Governor did not favour such a scheme. The women always fought and rioted the night before they were due for deportation. Why should they change now? They would injure each other if they were not chained and damage the coaches.

"You don't realise that these women always cause trouble at this time. They smash and damage everything they can," the Governor said, hoping that at last Elizabeth would agree with him.

"Then do as I suggest and perhaps there will be no more trouble," said Elizabeth. "You must change the way they are forced to travel in open waggons to the boat, jeered at by gangs at the roadside."

"Your suggestion won't work. The women prisoners will only cause trouble and try to escape."

"I can only repeat that whatever sentence these women have to serve we should treat them with kindness and humanity," said Elizabeth. "Send them in hackney-coaches with their turn-keys and I'll follow in my hackney and see them into the ship."

The Governor could argue no more. He had serious doubts about her suggestion but agreed to give it a try. So the next morning the women prisoners who were sentenced to transportation to Australia were put quietly in hackneys with their turnkey escorts. Elizabeth followed in her hackney. There were no jeering shouts from gangs of louts hanging about in the streets. They watched the hackney coaches go by in silent curiosity.

They had to go aboard the convict ship *Maria*

at Deptford. Women were arriving from other prisons. Some of these came by sea in fishing boats. Many were sick, cold and desperate with fear. Other arrived in open waggons, chained together. The women coming from Newgate in the closed hackney carriages arrived in better shape than the others.

Elizabeth, carrying her Bible, met her committee of ladies and went on board the ship to check on the conditions for the women. On this occasion there were 128 prisoners to be crowded below decks. At least this is what the ship's captain had expected, but Elizabeth and her ladies soon took over. They divided the women into groups and arranged for them to have sufficient space to lie down during the voyage, which would be a very long one.

Once the women convicts were settled, the reforming ladies went among them, distributing scraps of material. These could be used to make patchwork quilts which the convicts would be able to sell on arrival in Australia. The *Maria* was at anchor for two weeks and the ladies were able to make many visits to the ship to make sure that they had provided material, clothing and other items for all the women. In this way every women prisoner was made aware that Elizabeth and her ladies were concerned for them.

Just before the *Maria* was due to sail, Elizabeth went back to the ship to make her goodbye a special occasion. All the women were brought on deck to hear Elizabeth talk to them. Then she opened her Bible and read to them in her gentle, clear voice. The women listened in complete attention to everything she said and many sailors, including those high up in the ship's rigging, stopped work to listen.

Once Elizabeth had become involved in the welfare of women prisoners who were transported to Australia, she was their friend and helper for the rest of her life. During the next twenty years, she was often to be seen with her ladies, going aboard these ships. More than a hundred convict ships were visited and inspected by her over the years.

With only sailing ships to make the voyage to Australia, communication with New South Wales was slow and unreliable. So once the convict ships had sailed from Deptford, it was difficult to be sure how the women on board had been treated during the journey and when they arrived at the settlement in Australia. Elizabeth tried to have a matron appointed to each ship but without success. Then from 1815 it was agreed that a doctor should travel with each ship to check that conditions were clean and there was sufficient food.

Sometimes news would reach Britain that a convict ship had been wrecked at sea and lives had been lost, including those of children. Elizabeth was always badgering her friends in Parliament to improve the laws. Nothing was too much trouble for her when she was trying to achieve some improvements in the lives of women prisoners. One day she would go to see a member of the Government. The next day she would be putting her case to an admiral.

At last changes came in the laws. No woman being taken to a convict ship was to be chained, and if she had small children under the age of seven, she was allowed to take them with her to Australia. Gradually her efforts were bringing relief to prisoners who had suffered for so long from the horrible conditions involved in transportation. The publicity that Elizabeth achieved helped to make the people of Britain aware of the need for more humane treatment for prisoners.

All the time Elizabeth Fry was busy with all kinds of welfare programmes which often involved long and exhausting journeys by coach. She visited Newgate regularly, always talking and reading to the women from the Bible. Sometimes there were special guests. In July 1818, for example, she was accompanied by the Chancellor of the Exchequer, no doubt hoping for financial aid for one of her prison improvements.

In 1823 she was delighted when Robert Peel's Prison Act was passed in Parliament. This act appointed local justices to inspect prisons. They had to report to the Home Secretary if conditions were unsatisfactory. Elizabeth, during her own visits to prisons, kept a careful watch to see if the new laws were in fact being carried out. She published her own observations of years of visiting prisons. It was full of wise advice and was widely read not only in Britain but also abroad.

During these years she had become famous in Europe for her reforming Christian work. In Russia, an Englishman named Walter Venning was doing similar work in Russian prisons and they exchanged ideas by letter. Later the Russian Princess Sophia, hearing of Elizabeth's achievements in Britain, formed committees of ladies to visit Russian prisons.

Always ready to advise and help in such work, Elizabeth wrote letters, explaining her ideas on buildings for mentally ill people. She also described how she thought these people should be treated. Her suggestions included patience, kindness and giving the patients as much freedom as possible. Princess Sophia had Elizabeth's letters translated into Russian and many of her ideas became part of the Russian system in prisons at that time.

At home Elizabeth was always worried by the lack of concern for children. In many cases if the children's parents were in prison, there was no one to care for them properly. With so much poverty, unrest and cruelty around them, children could easily copy criminal habits and end up in trouble themselves.

In 1824 Elizabeth Fry opened a house for girls aged between seven and thirteen who had been convicted of some offence. Her aim was to reform them through work, education and the Bible. Teaching at the home was strict and the girls had to keep up good standards of behaviour.

Elizabeth believed that those who had committed serious crimes should be treated firmly but fairly. Some women prisoners who did not behave well were made to spend hours on a treadwheel. They had to keep walking on the wheel until they were exhausted. Elizabeth did not try to get the treadwheel abolished but she did campaign for it to be used only under supervision and only with women who had behaved exceptionally badly.

Up until the 1820s Joseph and Elizabeth Fry had been wealthy people with a fine home and many servants. Joseph owned and ran a bank. Without such wealth it would have been difficult, if not impossible, for Elizabeth to have achieved so much. However, there were now signs that Joseph would lose some of his money. Banks lent people money to invest and many people put this money into companies in South America that turned out to be useless. During 1825 many banks had to close down for this reason but for three years Joseph managed to stay in business. Then one day in November 1828 he told Elizabeth gravely, "My business is bankrupt."

7

JOSEPH IS BANKRUPT

TO be bankrupt in 1828 was not uncommon but Joseph Fry was a Quaker and for him to lose his business was a terrible blow. Quakers were supposed to be honest but careful and reliable business people. Elizabeth had been aware for some time of her husband's difficulties. She thought he was too free and easy in business matters but until then he had managed to survive, and she had been concentrating on many other things.

For a few days in November that year, they hoped the bank might be able to carry on, but the situation was too risky. No one would put money into the bank but everyone wanted to withdraw their savings. On 21 November the bank closed.

This meant that Joseph and Elizabeth had to watch bailiffs come to their home and make lists of everything they owned. These items were taken away to pay off some of the bank's debts.

Elizabeth's brothers and sisters were rich and did what they could to help, sending money and gifts. Poor Joseph was not so fortunate. The Society of Friends could no longer accept him as a member as he had let down their good name for sound business. Some friends such as William Wilberforce tried to encourage Elizabeth and

Joseph but it was a time of misery for them both.

People began to gossip about how Elizabeth had spent large amounts of money on charity. It was no wonder, they said, that the Fry family could not run their business properly. With so much feeling against him, Joseph did not want to go to the Society of Friends Meeting but Elizabeth thought that they should go.

"It will be hard for me to sit there when I know the members are accusing me of letting my business fail," said Joseph.

"It is difficult for us but I'm sure we should go," said Elizabeth.

So Joseph was persuaded to go. For some time they sat in the gallery in embarrassed silence. It was hard for Elizabeth to accept that God approved of the bad fortune they had suffered but when she spoke at the meeting, she told everyone that her faith in God was as strong as ever.

Three of Elizabeth's brothers helped to get Joseph's tea business in order and arranged for him to work for them. His income was much lower than before the collapse of his business and his family had to change their way of life. They were unable to afford to stay at Plashet and keep a staff of servants. It was a great shock to Elizabeth to have to leave this large house with its beautiful lawns, park and small farm.

Elizabeth's brother, Samuel Gurney, had been one of those who had helped to keep the family tea business going. Now he came to them with another offer of help. He owned a mansion in

West Ham called Ham House. Adjoining this was a smaller house called the Cedars in Upton Lane. It had pleasant, formal gardens with beautiful cedar trees. The house, built in the Queen Anne style, was of red brick and although it was not a mansion, it was a pleasant enough place to live.

"It would please me if you'd accept the Cedars as your home," said Samuel when Elizabeth and Joseph were discussing how they would miss Plashet after so many years.

"That is a kind and much appreciated offer, that we are glad to accept," said Joseph.

The Cedars was a pleasant enough home but Elizabeth felt sad the last time she wrote up her diary in her room at Plashet. They moved to the Cedars in June 1829. The effect of the worry and disappointments she had experienced had made Elizabeth ill and for a time she had to rest. They had lost a great deal of money but they had a nice home, four servants and could still live well. As soon as possible Elizabeth was busy once more at Quaker meetings and with her prison work.

When King William IV and Queen Adelaide were crowned in 1830 Elizabeth wished to meet them, hoping they would support her social work. She was not in such favour as in her wealthier times, however, and no invitation to meet either of the royal couple ever came. Elizabeth was determined that they should be reminded of the many social problems which needed urgent attention, so she sent Queen Adelaide her book on prison visiting and various papers on educating the poor, religion and the abolition of slavery.

Some of her ideas were losing support to those of such people as Edwin Chadwick, a young lawyer who believed that criminals should have shorter sentences, but that prisons should be harsher places. It was thought that the police should keep a check on ex-prisoners to make sure they did not again break the law. Chadwick thought that Elizabeth Fry's ideas for prisons gave the prisoners too easy a time and were too expensive to run.

The number of prisoners had risen from 35,000 in 1817 to 121,000 in 1831 and there was much anxiety about this great rise in crime. The following year Elizabeth appeared before a Committee of the House of Commons. She could tell at once that its members were unfriendly to her ideas.

"These things you've brought about such as work and payment for women prisoners, doesn't this make life too easy for them?" asked one member.

"I've been into many prisons and can tell you it does not," said Elizabeth. "Prisoners would prefer to play games and drink which is bad for them. By making them work you're giving them something useful to do and preparing them for life when they leave prison."

The Committee did not want to hear such talk. They wished to make prisons so dreadful that people would fear going to them and therefore would not dare to commit crimes. Elizabeth wanted prisons to try to make prisoners better people through useful work and a knowledge of the teachings of the Bible. When the Committee issued their report they ignored her evidence.

Elizabeth was disappointed at the report but this setback did not stop her continuing to work for the things in which she believed. In August 1832 she was in Southern Ireland and carried out an exhausting programme of preaching at Quaker meetings.

Her travels were continued next year when she went to the Channel Islands, visiting Sark, Herm, Guernsey and Jersey. She loved to wander round the streets of St Helier, in Jersey, visiting people in their cottages, talking to them and distributing the religious pamphlets that she always carried with her. She loved the green countryside with its rolling pastures and noticed with pleasure the lack of beggars and signs of poverty, compared with London.

Anything that involved a need for people interested her. In the Spring of 1834 she was in Freshwater on the Isle of Wight where she spent a pleasant day as a guest of the local coastguards. As usual she talked to them about religion and education for their children and was concerned when she discovered they had urgent need of a library.

"It's not only the coastguards of Freshwater who have no opportunity to read books," said Elizabeth when she was back home with Joseph.

"It's coastguards all over Britain. I'd like to create libraries for every coastguard station in the country."

"That's a fine idea and I will help you in any way I can," Joseph promised.

"We will appeal to people all over the country for money to buy books," said Elizabeth.

They soon found they had undertaken a great task. There were nearly five hundred coastguard stations in the country and to supply them all with even a small library would take an immense amount of time, money and hard work. That did not put off Joseph and Elizabeth. At every opportunity she spoke on behalf of the coastguards, explaining their needs. Joseph handled the correspondence to the many religious organisations.

The project took two years and during that time Elizabeth and Joseph were also busy with other work. In the end more than 52,000 books were supplied to the coastguards, and seamen in the British Navy also benefited.

In July 1836, Elizabeth, Joseph and their oldest daughter, Kate, left Southampton for the Channel Islands, not realising that their lives would soon be in danger. The sea was calm and the voyage seemed to be uneventful when suddenly the ship was surrounded by a swirling fog. The captain, uncertain of his position and worried by the dangerous rocks all around, stopped his ship, which began to drift. Both crew and passengers were fearful of what was going to happen.

"Stay with me," Elizabeth called to Kate and naturally her daughter did so but just at that moment there was an ominous grating sound as the hull of the ship scraped against some rocks. As the steamer started its engines and the paddles turned in an attempt to move it away from the rocks, Elizabeth called to a steward standing nearby.

"Bring us some coffee," she said and a few minutes later as they were drinking, they heard the sound of a voice through a loud speaker, telling them that they were approaching the Guernsey quayside.

It was a great relief to the three of them to go ashore on what was by then a sunny Sunday morning. Elizabeth Fry had been calm throughout the ordeal but as they walked on land and listened to the church bells ringing, she admitted to her daughter that she had not expected to see such a Sunday again.

While they were staying at Guernsey they received bad news that one of Elizabeth's sisters was ill. It was decided that she should return to England while Joseph Fry and his daughter went to France to visit the town of Rouen and the surrounding regions. Once again their lives were to be at risk.

On 21 September Joseph Fry and Kate had left Rouen in a carriage bound for Château Gaillard. Their route took them along some zig-zag roads that descended steep hills to the banks of the River Seine. They were sitting in the closed carriage when suddenly they were aware that it was swaying and jolting in a dangerous manner. The horses had broken into a mad gallop which the driver was struggling to control. Joseph Fry tried to open the carriage door.

"It's too late," he said. "We can't get out."

Kate's maid, who had accompanied them, was terrified and turned to her mistress for comfort as the horses bolted ever faster. There was little that Kate could do and when one horse slipped and fell, she could only cry out, "Lord have mercy on us."

The horses were galloping at full speed at the very edge of the road with a sheer drop to the river far below. Even Joseph Fry seemed to have lost his nerve as he anticipated death at any moment. Then suddenly the coach went over the edge and crashed down for more than thirty metres before it came to rest.

Some farm workers in a nearby orchard saw the accident and rushed to the battered carriage to help. They found three cut, bleeding and shocked people who were fortunate to be still alive. They were taken to the village of Romilly where a doctor attended to their injuries. Joseph sent a message to his son William to inform him of the accident.

"You're not to worry, they are all recovering well," William told his mother when he visited her on 2 October.

"At least that is good but I must go to see them," said Elizabeth.

So she crossed the Channel once again, going to Calais to greet her husband, daughter and the maid. She was thankful to find that their injuries had not been too serious. It was a relief to them all to arrive back home after visits to the Channel Islands and France that could have been tragic.

Elizabeth was soon active again in her work for the women prisoners of Newgate and especially for those who were being deported to Australia. Her brother-in-law, Fowell Buxton, was increasingly concerned about the suffering caused by slavery. Any human suffering disturbed Elizabeth Fry and she too was to be active on behalf of the anti-slavery movement.

8

ROYALTY LISTENS

IN June 1837 King William IV died and was succeeded by the young Queen Victoria. Elizabeth said prayers for the new queen and hoped she would be interested in social reform. It was a new reign with new ideas but these were not according to Elizabeth's beliefs.

"Still they come here knowing you will help them," said Joseph after a group of poor women had called at Upton to see Elizabeth.

"I am sure these people have a real need of our help," said Elizabeth. "But I will go to their homes this week to make sure."

They did indeed get the occasional beggar at their home who was not genuinely poor but had heard of their reputation for generosity. Elizabeth could not afford to be wasteful at this time but these women looked in great need of food and clothing. Her own children, although they were now grown up and in most cases married, were always willing to help her with her constant desire for welfare work.

A new generation of people of influence meant that she could no longer expect support from important people of power in Britain, but abroad she was still a famous name. Elizabeth feared that reforms she had worked for over the years could be lost as ideas changed.

She was happier in January 1838, however, when she went on a specially arranged religious visit to France with Joseph, Josiah Forster, a senior member of the Society of Friends and Lydia Irving, a young member of the Society. After a short stay in Boulogne, they journeyed on to Paris.

Here Elizabeth and her party were given a great welcome. It was assumed that she would want to visit prisons, hospitals and schools and arrangements were made for her to do so. At the women's prison of St Lazare, a thousand prisoners were assembled to listen to her. A translation of her talk was given to the women in French.

Everywhere she attracted crowds and friendly comment. Even the King of France, Louis Phillippe, and his queen were interested to meet her. She was able to give away copies of her books on prisons and also books by her daughter Louisa, on education. It was a wonderful visit to France and when Elizabeth returned home she did not miss opportunities to talk about it to Society of Friends audiences.

For the next few years she continued her round of visits and talks. In February 1840 she was granted a meeting with Queen Victoria and told the Queen how pleased she was that she encouraged many charities. That same month Elizabeth was off again on a tour of Belgium,

Holland and Germany. This time she went with her wealthy brother, Samuel Gurney, who was able to make sure that she enjoyed the best of everything during the journey.

She was listened to with great respect wherever she went. As usual she had government permission to visit prisons. She was able to present her opinions to the most important people, including princes, princesses, kings and queens. Six years previously she had taken a German pastor, named Fliedner, on a visit to Newgate Prison. He had talked to her about his ideas for improving the training of nurses. Now they met again in Germany in Kaiserwerth, an old town on the River Rhine.

"When I saw you in England, you inspired me with your work," said Pastor Fliedner, "Now you must come and see what happens in my training institutions."

Elizabeth was very happy to have the chance to visit the Kaiserwerth Institution. She found women being trained as teachers and nurses and was most impressed by everything she saw.

"There isn't time to try to improve everything in this world and much of my time has been concerned with the welfare of prisoners," she told the Pastor. "There should be training like this for nurses everywhere, including Britain. I will do my utmost to see that something is done."

Elizabeth returned to Britain in May and soon had plans for a training school for nurses. They had to serve in a hospital at first to see if they would be suitable for nursing, then they went on to Guy's Hospital for training. The young trainee nurses lived in a special home in London and were expected to spend some of their time nursing poor people. Fifteen years later, nurses who had trained under Elizabeth Fry's plan went to nurse wounded soldiers in the Crimean War with Florence Nightingale.

In 1833 a law abolishing slavery in the British Empire had been passed. This brought much joy to Elizabeth who for years had supported her brother-in-law, Fowell Buxton, and her friend William Wilberforce in their long fight against slavery. It was therefore no longer legal in the lands ruled by Britain to trade with slaves and ship them to the sugar plantations. But there were still European countries that allowed it. When the World's Anti-Slavery Convention was held in London the month after her European tour in 1840, Elizabeth was present.

In the same year Elizabeth's brother, Joseph, returned from America. His visit there had included a stay in the West Indies which had made him very opposed to slavery. When he went to Europe in July 1841 he invited his sister to go with him. She accepted and before long they were guests of the King and Queen of Denmark. Elizabeth discussed religious education with the king and Joseph took the opportunity to explain why he thought slavery should be abolished.

It was encouraging for her, at a time when some of her ideas were losing favour in Britain, to find so much support among the people of Europe. Crowds gathered to hear her speak or even just to see her, often bringing gifts of flowers and fruit. So much activity and travelling exhausted her, however, and she looked weak and ill when she arrived in England in October. For some months she had to rest, staying in the homes of her children.

In the middle of January 1842 she received an invitation from her friend, Lady Perie, wife of the Lord Mayor of London, to attend a special banquet at Mansion House in the City of London. This was in honour of Queen Victoria's husband, Prince Albert, who had come to lay the first stone of the Royal Exchange.

"Don't fuss," said Elizabeth when her husband suggested that she might not yet be well enough to attend such an occasion. "I feel much better and I don't want to miss this chance to remind the Prince about some of the things that need to be remedied in our prisons."

If he had known what was going to happen, Joseph would not have agreed that she should go. On a cold January afternoon she left Upton Lane in a coach with Samuel Gurney and a maid. When they reached the streets near the Mansion House there were large crowds and the roads were congested with carriages. In the confusion the driver of Elizabeth's coach took a wrong turning. Samuel Gurney looked anxiously through the coach window and realising that they were going the wrong way and it was getting late, he called to the driver to stop.

"We have to get to the Mansion House immediately," he said.

"I am sorry," replied the driver. "The roads are blocked and I can't get through."

Samuel looked at Elizabeth in her brown silk dress and then at the state of the weather and the roads outside. He stepped outside the coach and called to the footmen with them to help. Elizabeth had to join them in the street.

"I'm afraid there is nothing else we can do but try to walk through the crowd to the Mansion House," said Samuel.

The two footmen and Samuel did their best but the crowd pushed and shoved them until Elizabeth complained that she felt faint. Then Samuel saw two policemen and explained the situation to them. Even with the help of the policemen they had a great struggle to get through. By the time poor Elizabeth had reached the steps of the Mansion House, her dress was covered in mud and she was exhausted.

In the quiet luxurious atmosphere inside the Mansion House, though, Elizabeth soon recovered from her ordeal. It was an impressive setting for the dinner. There were beautiful flowers everywhere, and the big Venetian style room with its marble fireplaces and gilt ceilings was magnificent. The furniture in red satin and gold and the huge red carpet added to the occasion. Servants moved among the guests dressed in their finest clothes. The names of the guests were announced in ringing tones as they arrived.

"Mrs Fry!" a marshall called out.

The buzz of conversation stopped. Then the

City of London Sword Bearer appeared followed by the Mace Bearer. They in turn were followed by the Lord Mayor with Mrs Fry on his arm. The Mayor wore all his regalia of robes and jewels while Mrs Fry, a small figure by his side, wore her plain brown silk gown. They were met by the Mayoress. Eventually Elizabeth was able to rest on a sofa.

The banquet was a grand affair and Elizabeth sat between Sir Robert Peel and Prince Albert. The Duke of Wellington was also a guest as were other members of the Government. It was not long before Elizabeth was enjoying a pleasant conversation with the Prince.

"There is a great need for religious education," she told him. "I'm sure that even the royal children have this need."

"Of course," agreed the Prince. "We all have a need for religion including the royal children. They have the same problems when they first cut their teeth as do all children. But tell me about your most interesting visit to Europe."

"There I was able to discuss with King Christian and other royal princes the good and bad things I saw in the European prisons," she said.

"I hope after all your great work here, our prisons now compare well with those abroad," said the Prince.

"We have done some things for the better here but of late I think we are trying to be too harsh."

"I'm sorry to hear that you think that," said

the Prince. "Have you certain things in mind that you could tell me about?"

"The first thing is solitary confinement. I have always thought that making a human being exist alone is wrong." Elizabeth went on calmly but making sure her point was made. "We should try to make wrongdoers better but at the moment we think only of more severe punishments. Would you please tell her Majesty the Queen of my concern for these things."

The Prince promised that he would although he knew that the power to change laws was in the hands of the Government. So he changed the conversation to talking about Elizabeth's children and grandchildren.

Then it was time for the concluding speeches. There was a fanfare of trumpets, 'God Save the Queen' was played and the Prince made a speech, followed by Sir Robert Peel who said, "There is not a table in Europe who would not be honoured by the presence of Elizabeth Fry."

So Elizabeth was praised and treated with kindness and respect. It was recognised that Elizabeth had done fine work even though she was regarded as being rather old-fashioned, and she was thought by some to want to make prisons too pleasant for the prisoners.

At the end of January, Queen Victoria's eldest son was christened. He was one day to be King Edward VII. The King of Prussia, who had met Elizabeth during her tour of Europe, was one of the guests at the christening. He now let it be known he wished to see Elizabeth again, so she received an invitation to meet him at the Mansion House after the ceremony. The King was delighted to see her and when she told him she would be reading to the prisoners at Newgate in two days time, he said he would like to visit the prison on that occasion.

"Afterwards I would be delighted if you could be my guest for lunch at Upton," said Elizabeth.

"I too would be delighted to accept your invitation," said the King.

When the news of the visit was known there was much comment. The home of Joseph and Elizabeth was considered very ordinary as a place to entertain a king. Whatever was she thinking about making such an invitation when her brother's mansion, Ham House, was next door? Such comments, even from some of her own children, did not make Elizabeth change her mind. The king had wanted to come to her home and that was good enough for her.

So preparations went ahead and it was planned that all of Elizabeth's family should be there to meet the King of Prussia. On the Tuesday morning, Elizabeth was met at Newgate by the King, escorted by the Lady Mayoress and the sheriffs of London. Nearly thirty years ago she had entered this place for the first time wondering what reception she would receive from the dirty, underfed crowd of women prisoners. Now sixty prisoners, looking tidily dressed, assembled round her table to listen quietly while she read to them before a king, the mayoress, the sheriffs and many of her own committee of ladies. It was a wonderful moment which she would never forget as she concluded her reading of chapter 12 of Romans with prayers both for the women prisoners and the royal party.

She left Newgate by coach, accompanied by the mayoress and the sheriffs, ahead of the King and the royal party. Of course everyone at Upton knew about the royal visit. As Elizabeth approached her home, she could hear bells ringing and crowds cheering as she went by. The many poor children, for whom she had done so much, were standing by the church wall, adding their own cheers to the occasion.

Fortunately Elizabeth's coach was in good time. She was able to hurry indoors to take off her cloak. Then joined by her husband and seven of their sons and sons-in-law, they went to the entrance to meet the King's carriage as it arrived. Elizabeth escorted the King into her drawing-room which was beautifully decorated with flowers. Here she presented not only her own children but also her twenty-five grandchildren.

There followed a fine dinner. Elizabeth sat next to the King and was able to talk to him all the time. Everything was a great success and the King obviously enjoyed his visit for he stayed longer than had been planned.

By the spring of 1842, Elizabeth was ill and having to rest. When summer came she had not improved and went to stay by the sea at Cromer with her husband. In spite of her poor health, she carefully followed all the news about improvements in prisons and on convict ships. She was as aware as ever that so much still needed to be done, but she worried that her bad health might prevent her from carrying on with her work.

Even while she was supposed to be resting in Cromer, Elizabeth noticed the local fishermen had no kind of social club where they could meet. With Joseph's help, she organised the collection of contributions to build a rest room and library for the fishermen.

In April 1843 she went with her daughter Katherine on a visit to France. Her brother Joseph and his wife Eliza also came with them. Elizabeth visited prisons, went to Paris and there she met the King and Queen of France. When she left for home at the end of May, she was laden with presents from her many French friends.

Her previous visits to Europe were already bringing results. Through her talks with the King of Denmark, prisons in that country had been improved and new ones built; ladies committees in France were visiting prisoners and there were reports of improvements in the treatment of German prisoners. In Britain matrons were now to be appointed to all convict ships taking women prisoners to Australia.

By the end of July, that year, Elizabeth was tired and ill and Joseph took her to stay by the sea at Sandgate. She was unhappy and lacked her usual interest in people around her. One day she said she was tired of Sandgate and would like to visit her old home in Norwich.

"You need more rest before you're ready for such a long journey," said Joseph.

"I'm not happy here," Elizabeth insisted.

In the end Joseph took her to nearby Tunbridge Wells where her daughters Hannah and Louisa could help to nurse her. By October she was back home in Upton Lane but too ill to travel. In the Spring of the following year she was only able to sit in a wheel chair and be taken from room to room. This made her restless and ambitious to go farther.

"I would like to go to Bath to see everybody," she told Joseph. "I feel quite well enough to make the journey."

Bath was a lovely town, and Elizabeth so wanted a change, to see different scenery and people, so Joseph decided it would be better to go. They would travel on the mail coach which was the fastest and most comfortable way of getting to Bath even though steam railways would soon provide stiff competition.

In Bath Elizabeth enjoyed seeing her sister Hannah and her husband Fowell Buxton. Elizabeth's son William and his small daughter Emma also came to visit them. Seeing them all again was a great tonic to Elizabeth who eventually returned to Upton feeling better.

For a year she was able to be a little more active, to walk slowly and go out for drives in a pony carriage. Then at last, in the spring of 1845, she found the strength to take the coach to Norwich and visit her much loved old home of

Earlham Hall. She even managed two attendances at Quaker Meetings when she spoke to her old friends.

She greatly enjoyed her visit to Norwich and Joseph hoped that the happiness she felt would bring her better health. Unfortunately this did not happen. During the summer she rested at Ramsgate but she was too weak to find pleasure in the sunshine and beautiful views of the sea. Her health continued to get worse and she died on 13 October that year.

A crowd of more than a thousand people gathered at the Society of Friends Burial Ground in Barking when Elizabeth Fry was buried. They had come to pay their last respects to the lady of mercy and kindness who had spent her life, concerned for those who were suffering. By her determination and religious sense of purpose she had caused governments and royalty, in her own country and abroad, to share that concern.